HOW TO
TEACH READING
WITH
CHILDREN'S BOOKS

WORDS BY JEANNETTE VEATCH
PICTURES BY WARREN GOODRICH

Second Edition

RICHARD C. OWEN PUBLISHERS, INC. · NEW YORK

INTRODUCTION

With so many fine children's books now available, teachers have long needed more help in using them in **all** phases of their reading programs. Of course, the recreational reading period has long been with us, but much more than this can be done with children's books.

This booklet deals with the _instructional_ reading program and gives step-by-step helps to those teachers who want to expand their teaching of reading and place it upon a much broader literary base than has been usual in the past. The ideas presented are for the majority of American elementary classroom teachers — those with typical classes, ordinary equipment, and average skill, experience, and training.

We hope that this booklet will help the teacher-reader move into that state of Nirvana where all his pupils cannot be stopped from reading.

Jeannette Veatch

FIRST →

Elemental
Harvard Edu
Horn Book Ma
Journal of Lea
Journal of Readin
Journal of Readin
Reading Research Q
Reading Teacher
Review of Educatio

If you locate artl
with me as to appr

B) Group Presenta

The second a
involve you in wor
your peers. These
some degree it will
You are to ass
You have been aske
to parents at your
Working with y
can synthesize and
have gathered in y
ten minute oral pre
21.

We will
attention   upon
questions   and d.
to   share   your   wr
class   as   a   whole.
entry   or   when   you
it completely and jus

Your   journals
the   semester,   so   t
to   see   that   you   a
of   entries.   I   will
the   Quad   (October
way,   based   upon   th
the entries and the '
made. As you can see
content, so you can
in a free and persor
is   that   the   journal
involvement with   the

Journal   writir
seriously and work ha
journals   should   hel;
more   meaningful   and
enjoy writing!

7. Master the b.
8. Demonstrate t.
   teaching of a .

II) <u>Texts</u>

   Burns, Roe and Ross
      <u>School</u>. Boston

   Smith, Frank. <u>Read</u>
      College Press,

   Various professiona
   the Curriculum Libra

III) <u>Course Requirements</u>:

   1. Readings and Clas

      Readings will
   textbooks and select
   readings <u>prior</u> to t
   that reading. In thi
   part in class activit
   reading will be essen
   described below.

The articles read shoul⟨ ⟩
journals.

a. Write an annotated biblio⟨ ⟩
each article identified as "n⟨ ⟩
sentences identify the main p⟨ ⟩
the information it contains c⟨ ⟩

b. Each summary and evaluat⟨ ⟩
double spaced and more than o⟨ ⟩

GET LOTS OF BOOKS!

BIG books, little books, paperbacks, **FAT** books, THIN books, FAIRY stories, **COWBOY** stories, MYSTERIES, SiLLY stories...

...ANY BOOKS THAT YOUR PUPILS WILL LIKE AND BE ABLE TO READ.

WHERE ??? YOU'D BE SURPRISED!

... the librarian, the PTA, classroom book club, your supervisor, your principal, yes, even THE SCHOOL BOARD !.........

... be ingenious !

Research in the attic ...

Buy 'em...

Swap 'em...

Hunt for 'em anywhere ...

Order 'em ...

Fight for 'em ...

Borrow 'em ....

Read 'em yourself if you like .

GET AT **LEAST** A HUNDRED BOOKS! MORE IF YOU CAN —
about three books for every pupil - three different ones, that is —

FIX UP A NICE PLACE FOR THE BOOKS,
available, spread out face up more than piled up —
no special order needed except maybe very general
headings . . .

old rug for belly whopping

OR→

A WALL RACK

SET UP a NICE QUIET PLACE
FOR YOURSELF WHERE IT'S PRIVATE ... BUT
WHERE YOU CAN STILL
SEE ALL . . . .

the READING PERIOD BEGIN
CAN NOW

ON DECK
OR
PRACTICE
CHAIRS

THE READING PERIOD

1. Teach children how to choose books wisely.

Use *RULE of THUMB* —

Choose a middle page with a lot of words.

Read silently. If you come to a word you don't know, put down your thumb. If you find another, put down your first finger, etc.

If you use up all your fingers the book is too hard, so put it back and try another.

BE SURE YOU LIKE THE BOOK!

2. Teach children to get books and read them without disturbing others.

3. Teach children how to get the help they need without disturbing others.

THEY CAN GO TO:

DICTIONARIES, EXPERIENCE CHARTS, CLASS NEWSPAPERS . . .

OTHER BOOKS WHICH THEY KNOW (*BOOKS ARE FRIENDS*) . . .

THE DAY'S WORD HELPER, TO THE TEACHER, OR TO A FRIEND . . . .

OR THEY CAN FIGURE IT OUT FROM CONTEXT, FROM A PICTURE, FROM THE BEGINNING SOUND.

it is also LEGAL to GUESS.. especially when it is a good story!

4. Teach them how to prepare a story for YOU.

TELL THEM TO :

I'M READY! THIS WILL BE THE **BEST READING** YOU EVER HEARD!

DECIDE ON WHICH STORY IT SHALL BE . .

READ IT TO THEMSELVES, AT LEAST TWICE

READ IT ALOUD, SOFTLY TO A FRIEND ——

IN SHORT, THEY MUST KNOW IT UNDER

HAVE THEM LIST THEIR NAMES FOR AN
INDIVIDUAL CONFERENCE

Susan
John
Donald
Joan

Louise

Mary
George

When everyone is reading his chosen book and all is quiet, peaceful, serene, hardworking . . .

IT IS TIME FOR →

THE INDIVIDUAL

... FIRST ONE ON THE LIST COMES TO YOU

PRIVATE CONFERENCE

SIDE BY SIDE

IN TEN MINUTES AND EVEN <u>FIVE</u> MINUTES FIND OUT :

THE MAIN IDEA AND STORY PLOT

THE CHILD'S INTEREST IN HIS BOOK

HOW THE READER SEES THE VALUES IN THE BOOK —

AS TO WHY THE AUTHOR WROTE IT — WHAT DOES IT

TELL ABOUT OUR WORLD . . .

and then, GLORY ! —

HOW WELL HE READS ALOUD!

CONFERENCE

THEN YOU :

KEEP A RECORD OF HIS PERFORMANCE IN YOUR CARD FILE OR NOTEBOOK

MAKE GROUP OR INDIVIDUAL ASSIGNMENT TO CORRECT A CERTAIN DIFFICULTLY

APPROVE A FURTHER PROJECT RELATED TO AN INTEREST, OR ANOTHER TYPE OF FOLLOW-UP —

SEND HIM BACK AND TAKE THE NEXT —

ALL THIS IN <u>FIVE MINUTES</u> — *HONEST!*

PRACTICE ON RAPID-FIRE QUESTIONS — YOU'LL MAKE IT — JUST TRY!

I CAN'T !
(SOB)
I CAN'T !

YOU CAN SO! <u>LOTS</u> OF TEACHERS HAVE !

...meanwhile the REST of the CLASS is having an

INDEPENDENT WORK PERIOD
(all's quiet on the seatwork front)

MAJOR JOB :

      READING THE CHOSEN CHILDREN'S BOOK

SUB-CONTRACTS :

      PRACTICING TO READ TO THE TEACHER

      DOING AN **ORIGINAL FOLLOW-UP** OF
      SOMETHING READ ------

                                                  SUCH AS

A CLASS NEWSPAPER . . .

...KEEPING TRACK OF BOOKS

JUST A LITTLE BIT OF
BUTTER FOR MY BREAD —

... CHORAL SPEAKING . . . .

... DRAMATIZATION . . . .
(getting ready for it, that is)

...and **LETTERS.!!** dozens of letters, hundreds of letters, thousands and millions and trillions of letters —

WRITE 'EM, LICK 'EM, STICK 'EM*

LETTERS TO:

THE PRESIDENT

THE ARMY, NAVY, AIR FORCE, MARINES

GRANDMA and GRANDPA

EARL, who's sick

SUSIE, who moved

JONES' DEPARTMENT STORE

The dairy, the laundry, etc., etc.

and to the UN

*stamp money from the Principal's petty cash —

... *CREATIVE WRITING*
singly or maybe an accumulative story book —

... *NEWS* —
discussion, argument, prognostication

...HUNDREDS OF INDEPENDENT ACTIVITIES...

WORKBOOKS
KEEP OUT!

HOBBIES
SCIENCE EXPERIMENTS
MODEL BUILDING
RESEARCH
CRAFTS —

READING *READING* READING

and more

READING!

While your cherubs are so busy, YOU are

FREE!.. to do what?

TEACH MORE READING!

GO BACK OVER THE RECORDS OF THE
INDIVIDUAL CONFERENCES — STUDY THEM.

EVERY WEEK MOST OF THE CHILDREN SHOULD
HAVE WORKED ALONE WITH YOU TWICE!

ASK YOURSELF:

- WHICH ONES HAVE THE SAME READING PROBLEM?
  CALL THEM TO YOU AS A GROUP —
  WORK OUT THAT DIFFICULTY —

- WHO ELSE HAS A SIMILAR PROBLEM?

Group and regroup according to INSTRUCTIONAL NEEDS —

Do this as often as you can find similar

NEEDS, INTERESTS or
DIFFICULTIES . . . .

GROUPING IS A <u>FAST</u> WAY TO TEACH THE
SAME SKILL TO A LOT OF PUPILS AT THE
SAME TIME, WHEN YOU ARE <u>SURE</u> THEY
NEED THAT SKILL . . . .

HAVE WHOLE CLASS SESSIONS —

- FOR ANY KINDS OF PLANNING
- FOR ANY KIND OF SHARING WHERE AN AUDIENCE IS NEEDED

- WHEN COOPERATION IS NEEDED TO GET SOMETHING DONE

   ✓ Assembly programs
   ✓ Safety Patrol Problems
   ✓ Decorating the room
   ✓ Helping the P-TA

CHILDREN'S BOOKS
are NICE BECAUSE :

They deal with ONE IDEA or CONCEPT

They are the product of CREATIVE ARTISTS

No one HAS to read them

Each is meant for a special reader – YOU ?

They have a point of view – you can take it or leave it

They sink or swim on their charm

They are beloved but *force feeding makes them hated.*

Let no teacher put CHILDREN'S BOOKS *aside* —

USE THEM , *whole loaf*

- ○ FOR READING INSTRUCTION
- ○ TO LEARN ABOUT THE WORLD of BOOKS
- ○ TO ENJOY THE RICHES of the WORLD'S STORY LORE in LITERATURE

TO READ IS TO THINK IS TO BECOME EDUCATED.

Where to look for greater detail.

Veatch, Jeannette. *"Reading in the Elementary School,"* New York: Richard C. Owen, Rockefeller Center, Box 819, N.Y. 10185, 1978.

Veatch, Jeannette, Sawicki, Florence, Geraldine Elliot, Eleanor Flake, Janice Blakey. *"Key Words to Reading,"* Columbus, Ohio: C.E. Merrill. 2nd Edition, 1979.

GOLDEN OLDIES — if you can find 'em.

Barbe, Walter B. *"Educator's Guide to Personalized Reading Instruction."* Englewood Cliffs, N.J.: Prentice-Hall. 1961

Barbe, Walter B. & Jerry L. Abbott, *"Personalized Reading Instruction: Techniques That Increase Reading Skill and Comprehension."* West Nyack, N.Y.: Parker Pub. Co. 1975

Burrows, Alvina Treut, *"Teaching Children in the Middle Grades,"* Boston: D.C. Heath, 1952. pp. 165-199.

Darrow, Helen Fisher and Virgil M. Howes, *"Approaches to Individualized Reading."* New York: Appleton-Century-Croft. 1960.

Dolch, Edward W. *"Individualized Reading Vs Group Reading."* ELEMENTARY ENGLISH, December 1961 & January 1962.

Draper, Marcella K. & Schwietert, Louise H. *"A Practical Guide to Individualized Reading."* New York. Board of Education, Bureau of Educational Research. Publication #40, 1960

Jacobs, Leland, et al., *"Individualizing Reading Practice."* New York: Teachers College Press, 1958.

Veatch, Jeannette, *"Individualizing Your Reading Program."* New York: G.P. Putnam's Sons. 1959.

Cassette Tapes:

Veatch, Jeannette, "*Individualized Reading*". Hollywood. Listener Corporation. 1970.

Good Magazine Articles.

Dunn, Rita, "*Another Look at Individualized Instruction.*" PHI DELTA KAPPAN February, 1978. PP. 400-402

Holdaway, Don "*Shared Book Experience: Teaching Reading Using Favorite Books.*" THEORY IN PRACTICE. The Ohio State University, Autumn, 1982.

Lazar, May. "*Individualized Reading: A Dynamic Approach.*" READING TEACHER. I.R.A. December 1957. pp. 75-82.

Thompson, Richard, "*Individualized Reading. A Summary of Research,*" EDUCATIONAL LEADERSHIP, A.S.C.D. Oct.1975.